God's Grandmother: Saint Anne

Brian Kiczek, D.C.

God's Grandmother: Saint Anne

Copyright © 2019 Brian Kiczek, D. C. – All rights reserved.
Cover Design: Sarah Kiczek
Published by My Catholic Family Magazine
"Strengthening the Family"
MyCatholicFamilyMagazine.com

All rights reserved. No part of this work may be reproduced, stored in a retrieval system, or submitted in any form or by any means, electronic, mechanical, photocopying, recording or otherwise, without the prior written permission of the publisher. This book may not be lent, resold, hired out or otherwise disposed of by way of trade in any form of binding or cover other than that in which it is published, without the prior written consent of the publisher
.
Printed in the United States of America.

This book is dedicated to all those who need devotion to Saint Anne especially those who read this book. May we all be worthy Grandchildren to so wonderful a Grandmother!

Foreword

In writing this book, I wish to kindle a great devotion to Saint Anne and to realize that she wants to be our heavenly grandmother. The first part of the book was adapted from the private revelations of Venerable Mary Agreda and Catherine Emmerich. These "private revelations" are not to be considered historical biography, but as Father Delehaye S.J stated in regards to the writings of Emmerich, "Let them read (Emmerich's writings) as a religious novel, but not as a fifth Gospel."

For more information about the differences between Private and Public revelations I recommend reading: catholic.com/tracts/private-revelation and "The Life of Mary as seen by the Mystics" which gives wonderful explanations in regards to it as well as the information and history of Venerable Mary Agreda.

The rest of the book gives us the history of devotion to Saint Anne, Shrine of Miracles, powerful prayers to Saint Anne as well as a chapter on Prayer and on Grandparents.

TABLE OF CONTENTS

1. The Marriage of St. Anne and St. Joachim............6

2. St. Anne and St. Joachim's Prayers are Answered…..19

3. How St. Anne and St. Joachim Obtained God's Grace to Conceive a Child…………………………..41

4. St. Anne Fulfills her Promise of Giving Mary to the Temple……………………………………………...52

5. The Deaths of St. Anne and St. Joachim….….….61

6. Devotion to St. Anne throughout the Ages…...71

7. Saint Anne de Beaupre Shrine: A Place of Miracles…………………………………………….83

8. Prayers to St. Anne…………………….....…..98

9. Prayer…..……………………………….…..104

10. Grandparents……………………………….131

Notes/Bibliography………………………….138

Chapter 1

THE MARRIAGE OF ST. ANNE AND ST. JOACHIM

"You are the one, who is specially blessed by God and whom He wishes to visit and enrich with more singular blessings."
~Angel to Saint Anne

Saint Anne was a pure, humble, and beautiful woman. From her childhood she led a most virtuous, holy life, enjoying many graces from God. She was always very diligent and industrious, and attained perfection in both the active and contemplative life. She was very knowledgeable of the divine Scriptures and had a profound understanding of its hidden mysteries and sacraments. In the infused virtues of faith, hope and love she was unequalled. Equipped with all these gifts, she continued to pray for the coming of the Messiah. Her prayers were very acceptable to the Lord.

Therefore, without doubt, Saint Anne holds a high position among the saints of the Old

Testament, who by their merits hastened the coming of the Redeemer.

Her future husband Saint Joachim, a holy man and illumined by special grace and light from on high, had a knowledge of many mysteries of the Holy Scriptures and of the Prophets. In continual and fervent prayer he asked of God for the fulfillment of His promises, and his faith and charity penetrated the heavens. He was also a very humble, holy, and pure man.

Saint Anne also prayed fervently, that the Almighty would answer her prayer for a good husband, who would help her to get closer to God. Their prayers were heard by God at the same time and answered. The archangel Gabriel was sent to announce it to them both. To Anne he appeared in visible form, while she was praying fervently for the coming of the Savior. When she saw the archangel, she was frightened and yet at the same time interiorly rejoiced. She prostrated herself in profound humility to reverence the messenger of heaven; but he prevented and encouraged her, as being destined to be the ark of the true manna, Mary most holy, Mother of the Word. The Archangel Gabriel said:

"The Most High gives you His blessing, servant of God, and be your salvation. His Majesty has heard your prayers and He wishes you to persevere and continue to pray for the coming of the Redeemer. It is His will, that you accept Joachim as your spouse, for he is a man of upright heart and acceptable to the Lord: together you will be able to persevere in the observance of God's law and in His service. Continue your prayers and supplications, for the Lord will see them fulfilled. Continuing to pray for the Messiah, be joyful in the Lord, who is your salvation."

With these words the angel disappeared, leaving her comforted and renewed in spirit.

To Saint Joachim, the archangel did not appear in a bodily form, but he spoke to him in sleep as follows:

"Joachim, be blessed by the right hand of the Most High! Persevere in thy desires and live according to perfection. It is the will of the Almighty that you receive Anne as your spouse, for the Lord has visited her with His blessing. Take care of her and esteem her as a pledge of the Most High and give thanks to His Majesty, because He has given her in your charge."

In consequence of this divine message Joachim immediately asked for the hand of the Anne and, in joint obedience to the divine ordainment, they espoused each other. But neither told each other the secret of what had happened until several years afterwards. The two holy spouses lived in Nazareth, continuing to walk with the Lord. In sincerity they practiced all virtue in their works, making themselves very acceptable and pleasing to the Most High and avoiding all sin in all their doings. Every year, the rents and incomes of their estate, they divided them into three parts. The first one they offered to the temple of Jerusalem for the worship of the

Lord; the second they distributed to the poor, and the third they retained for decent sustenance of themselves and family. God increased their temporal goods on account of their generosity and charity. They themselves lived with each other in undisturbed peace and union of heart, without quarrel or grudges. The most humble Anne subjected herself and conformed herself in all things to the will of Joachim: and that man of God, with equal imitation of humility, sought to know the desires of holy Anne, confiding in her with his whole heart, and he was not deceived. Thus they lived together in such perfect charity, that during their whole life they never experienced a time, during which one ceased to seek the same thing as the other. But rather as being united in the Lord, they enjoyed His presence in holy fear. Joachim, mindful to obey the command of the angel, honored his spouse and lavished his attention upon her.

This fortunate couple passed twenty years of their married life without having a child. In those times and among the people of the Jews this was held to be the greatest misfortune and disgrace. On this account they had to bear many criticisms and insults from their neighbors and acquaintances, since they were childless they were considered excluded from the benefits of the Messiah. But the Most High wished to afflict them and dispose them for the grace which awaited them, in order that in patience and submission they might tearfully sow the glorious fruit, which they were afterwards to bring forth. They continued to pray fervently from the bottom of their hearts. They made a vow to the Lord, that if He should give them a child, they would consecrate her/him to His service in the temple of Jerusalem.

Having, at the command of the Lord, persevered a whole year in fervent petitions, it happened by divine inspiration and ordainment, that Joachim was in the temple of Jerusalem offering prayers and sacrifices for the coming of the Messiah, and for the fruit, which he desired. Arriving with others of his town to offer the common gifts and contributions, however, a priest, harshly reprehended the old and venerable Joachim, for presuming to come with the other people to make offerings in spite of his being childless. Among other things he said to him:

"Why do you, Joachim, come with your offerings and sacrifices, which are not pleasing in the eyes of God, since you are a useless man. Leave immediately; do not annoy God with thy offerings and sacrifices, which are not acceptable to Him."

The holy man, full of shame and confusion, in humble love thus addressed the Lord:

"Most high Lord and God, at your command and desire I came to the temple; he that takes thy place, despises me; my sins merit this disgrace; but since I accept it according to your will, do not cast away the creature of your hands".

Joachim hurried away from the temple full of sorrow, though peaceful and contented, to a farm, which he possessed, and there in solitude he called upon the Lord for some days. While Joachim was making his prayers, a holy angel appeared to Anne, that her prayer for a child, accompanied by such holy desires and intentions, was pleasing to the Almighty. Rejoicing, she prayed with humble subjection and confidence, that God's will be fulfilled:

"Most high God, my Lord, Creator and Preserver of the universe, whom my soul reveres as the true God, infinite, holy and eternal! Prostrate in your real presence I will speak, though I am but dust and ashes proclaiming my need and my affliction. Lord God uncreated, make us worthy of thy benediction, and give us holy fruit of the womb, in order that we may offer it to thy service in the temple. Remember, O Lord, that Anne, your servant, the mother of

Samuel, was sterile and that by your generous mercy she received the fulfillment of her desires. I feel within me a courage which inspires me to ask You to show me the same mercy. Hear then, O sweetest Lord and Master, my humble petition: remember the sacrifices, offerings and services of my ancestors and the favors. I wish to offer, O Lord, a sacrifice pleasing and acceptable in your eyes: but the greatest in my power, is my soul, and my whole being. Look upon me from your throne giving me a child, I will from this moment sanctify and offer it for your service in the temple. Lord God of Israel, if it should be your pleasure and good will to look at this lowly and impoverished creature, and console your servant, Joachim, grant me my prayer and may I in all things be fulfilling thy holy and eternal will."

The petitions of the most holy Joachim and Anne reached the throne of the holy Trinity, where they were accepted and the will of God was made known to the holy angels.

The Angel Gabriel said to Anne:

"The humility, faith and the alms of Joachim and of yourself have come before the throne of the Most High and now He sends me, His angel, in order to give you news full of joy for your heart: His Majesty wishes, that you be most fortunate and blessed. He chooses you to be the mother of her who is to conceive and bring forth the only begotten of the Father. You shall bring forth a daughter, who by divine will shall be called MARY. She shall be blessed among women and full of the Holy Ghost. She shall be the cloud that shall drop the dew of heaven for the refreshment of mortals, and in her shall be fulfilled the prophecies of your ancestors. She shall be the portal of life and salvation for the sons of Adam. Know also that I have announced to Joachim, that he shall have a daughter who shall be blessed and fortunate: but the full knowledge of the mystery is not given him by the Lord, for he does not know, that she is to be the Mother of the Messiah. Therefore you must guard this secret; and go now to the temple to give thanks to the Most High for having been so highly favored by His powerful right hand. In the Golden Gate you shalt meet Joachim. **You are the one, who is specially blessed by God and whom He wishes to visit and enrich with more singular blessings.** In solitude God will speak to your heart and there give a beginning to the law of grace, since in your womb He will give being to her, who is to give the Immortal, mortal flesh and human form. In this humanity, united with the Word, will be written, as with His own blood, the true law of Mercy."

In order that the humble heart of the holy Anne might not faint away with admiration and joy at the news of the holy angel, she was strengthened by the Holy Spirit and thus she heard it and received it with great joy. Immediately arising she rushed to the temple of Jerusalem, and there found Joachim, as the angel had foretold to them both. Together they gave thanks to the Almighty for this wonderful blessing and offered special gifts and sacrifices. They were enlightened again by the grace of the Holy Spirit, and, full of divine consolation, they returned to their home. Joyfully they conversed about the favors, which they had received from the Almighty, especially concerning each one's message of the archangel Gabriel, whereby, on behalf of the Lord, they had been promised a daughter who should be most blessed and fortunate. Again they made the vow to offer their child to the temple and that each year on this day they would come to the temple to offer special gifts, spend the day in praise and thanksgiving, and give many alms. This vow they fulfilled to the end of their lives, spending this day in great praise and exaltation of the Most High.

  The prudent Anne never disclosed the secret that her Daughter was to be the Mother of the Messiah, either to Joachim or to any other person. Nor did Joachim in the course of his life know any more than that she was to be a grand and mysterious woman. However, in the last moments of his life the Almighty made the secret known to him.

Chapter 2

ST. ANNE AND ST. JOACHIM'S PRAYERS ARE ANSWERED

"We select for the formation of our beloved Mary the womb of our servant Anne; in her be she conceived and in her let that most blessed Soul be created."
~Most Holy Trinity

"Now the time has arrived," said the Holy Trinity, "for bringing to light the woman most pleasing and acceptable to our eyes. That woman, in whom the human nature is freed from its first sin, who is to crush the head of the dragon, who appeared in the heavens in our presence, and who is to clothe the Eternal Word with human flesh. The hour is at hand, so blessed for mortals, in which the treasures of Our Divinity are to be opened and the gates of heaven to be unlocked. Let the rigor of Our justice be softened by the chastisements, which we have until now executed upon the mortals; let the attribute of Our mercy become manifest; let the creatures be enriched, and let the Divine Word merit for them the treasures of grace and of eternal glory."

"Now let the human race receive the Repairer, the Teacher, the Brother and Friend, to be life for mortals, a medicine for the sick, a consoler for the sorrowful, a ointment for the wounded, a guide and companion for those in difficulties. Let now the prophecies of our servants and the promises made to them that We would send a Savior to redeem them, be fulfilled. We select for the formation of our beloved Mary the womb of our servant Anne."

The Almighty created the soul of His Mother and infused it into the body; and thus entered into the world that pure creature, more holy, perfect and agreeable to His eyes than all those He had created, or will create to the end of the world, or through the eternities.

By the force of this divine pronouncement and through the love with which it issued from the mouth of the Almighty, was created and infused into the body of most holy Mary her most blessed soul. At the same time she was filled with grace and gifts above those of the highest seraphim of heaven, and there was not a single instant in which she was found wanting or deprived of the light, the friendship and love of the Creator, or in which she was touched by the stain or darkness of original sin. On the contrary she possessed the most perfect justice, superior to that of Adam and Eve in their first formation. To her was also concealed the most perfect use of the light of reason, corresponding to the gifts of grace, which she had received. Not for one instant was she to remain idle, but to engage in works most admirable and pleasing to her Maker.

The happiest mother, holy Anne passed the days of her pregnancy altogether spiritualized by the divine operations and by the sweet workings of the Holy Spirit in all her faculties. Divine Providence, however, in order to direct her course to greater merit and reward, ordained, that the weight of trouble be not wanting, for without it the cargo of grace and love is scarcely ever secure. In order to understand better, what happened to this holy woman, it must be remembered, that Satan after he was hurled with the other bad angels from heaven into the infernal torments, never ceased, during the reign of the old Law, to search through the earth hovering with lurking vigilance above the women of distinguished holiness, in order to find her, whose sign he had seen and whose heel was to bruise and crush his head. Lucifer's wrath against men was so fierce, that he would not trust this investigation to his inferiors alone; but leaving them to operate against the virtuous women in general, he himself attended to this matter and assiduously hovered around those, who signalized themselves more particularly in the exercise of virtue and in the grace of the Most High.

  Filled with malice and astuteness, he observed closely the exceeding great holiness of

Anne and all the events of her life; and although he could not estimate the richness of the treasure, which was enclosed in her blessed womb (since the Lord has concealed this as well as many mysteries from him), yet he felt a powerful influence proceeding from Saint Anne. The fact that he could not penetrate into the source of this activity, threw him at times into greater fury and rage. At other times he quieted himself with the thought, that this pregnancy arose from the same causes as others in the course of nature and that there was no special cause for alarm; for the Lord left him to his own hallucinations and to the vagaries of his own fury. Nevertheless the whole event was a source of great troubles to this perverse spirit, when he saw how quietly her pregnancy took its course and especially, when he saw, that many angels stood in attendance. Above all he was enraged at his weakness in resisting the force, which proceeded from the blessed Anne and he suspected that it was not she alone, who was the cause of it.

Filled with this mistrust, the dragon determined, if possible, to take the life of the happy mother; or, if that was impossible, to see that she should obtain little satisfaction from her pregnancy. For the pride of Lucifer was so boundless as to persuade him of his ability to overcome or take away the life of her, who was to be the Mother of the Incarnate Word, or even the life of the Messiah and Redeemer of the world, if only he could obtain knowledge of their whereabouts. His arrogance was founded upon the superiority of his angelic nature to the condition and power of mere human nature; as if both were not subject to grace and entirely dependent upon the will of their Creator. Audaciously therefore he set himself to tempt holy Anne, with many suggestions, misgivings, doubts and diffidence about the truth of her pregnancy, alleging her protracted years. All this the demon attempted in order to test the virtue of the saint, and to see, whether these temptations would not afford some opening for the perversion of her will.

But the invincible matron resisted these onslaughts with humble fortitude, patience, continued prayer and vivid faith in the Lord. She brought to naught the perplexing lies of the dragon and on account of them gained only additional grace and protection from on high. For besides the protection abundantly merited by her past life she was defended and freed from the demons by the great princes, who were guarding her most holy daughter. Nevertheless in his insatiable malice the enemy did not desist on that account; and since his arrogance and pride far exceeds his powers, he sought human aid; for with such help he always promises himself greater ease of victory. Having at first tried to overthrow the dwelling of Saint Joachim and Anne, in order that she might be frightened and excited by the shock of its fall, but not being able to succeed on account of the resistance of the holy angels, he incited against Anne one of the foolish women of her acquaintance to quarrel with her. This the woman did with great fury, insolently attacking Anne with reproach and scorn; she did not hesitate to make mockery of her pregnancy, saying, that she was the sport of the demon in being thus found pregnant at the end of so many years and at so great an age. The blessed Anne did not permit herself to be disturbed by this attack, but in all meekness and humility bore the injuries and treated her assailants with kindness. From that time on she looked with greater love upon these women and lavished upon them so much the greater benefits. But their wrath was not immediately pacified, for the demon had taken possession of them, filling them with hate against the saint; and, as any concession to this cruel tyrant always increases his power over his victims, he incited these miserable dupes to plot even against the person and life of Saint Anne. But they could not put their plots into execution, because divine power interfered to foil their natural womanly weakness. They were not only powerless against the saint, but they were overcome by her admonitions and brought to the knowledge and amendment of their evil course by her prayers. The dragon was repulsed, but not vanquished; for he immediately availed himself of a servant, who lived in the house with Joachim and Anne, and exasperated her against the holy matron. Through her he created even a greater annoyance than through the other women, for she was a domestic enemy and more stubborn and dangerous than the others. I will not stay to describe, what the enemy attempted through this servant, since it was similar to that of the other woman, only more annoying and malicious. But with the help of God, Anne won a more glorious victory than before; for the watcher of Israel slumbered not, but guarded His holy City and furnished it so well with sentinels, chosen from the strongest of His hosts, that they put to ignominious flight Lucifer and his followers. No more were they allowed to molest the fortunate mother, who was already expecting the birth of the most blessed Princess of heaven, and who, enriched by heroic acts of virtue and many merits in these conflicts, had now arrived at the fulfillment of all her highest wishes.

    The day destined for the birth of her, who was consecrated and sanctified to be the Mother of God, had arrived: a day most fortunate for the world. This birth happened on the eighth day of September, fully nine months having elapsed since the conception of the soul of our most holy Queen and Lady. Saint Anne was prepared by an interior voice of the Lord, informing her, that the hour of delivery had come. Full of the joy of the Holy Spirit at this information, she prostrated herself before the Lord and sought the assistance of His grace and His protection for a happy deliverance. The most blessed child Mary was at the same time by divine providence and power ravished into a most high ecstasy. Hence Mary was born into the world without perceiving it by her senses, for their operations and faculties were held in suspense.

She was born pure and stainless, beautiful and full of grace, thereby demonstrating, that she was free from the law and the tribute of sin. Although Mary was born substantially like other daughters of Adam, yet her birth was accompanied by such circumstances and conditions of grace that it was the most wonderful and miraculous birth in all creation and will eternally redound to the praise of her Maker. At twelve o'clock in the night this divine luminary issued forth, dividing the night of the ancient Law and its pristine darkness from the new day of grace, which now was about to break into dawn. She was clothed, handled and dressed like other infants, though her soul dwelt in the Divinity; and she was treated as an infant, though she excelled all mortals and even all the angels in wisdom. Her mother did not allow her to be touched by other hands than her own, but she herself wrapped Mary in swaddling clothes:

and in this Anne was not hindered by her present state of childbirth; for she was free from the toils and labors, which other mothers usually endure in such circumstances.

Saint Anne received in her arms her daughter, the most exquisite treasure of all the universe, inferior only to God and superior to all other creatures. With fervent tears of joy she offered this treasure to His Majesty, saying interiorly "Lord of infinite wisdom and power, Creator of all that exists, this fruit of my womb, which I have received of your bounty, I offer to you with eternal thanks, for without any merit of mine you have given it to me. Look down upon our lowliness from your exalted throne. Be eternally blessed, because you have enriched the world with a child so pleasing to your bounty and you have prepared a dwelling–place and a tabernacle for the eternal Word. I offer congratulations to my holy forefathers and to the holy Prophets, and in them to the whole human race, for this sure pledge of Redemption, which you have given them. But how shall I be able to worthily to treat her, whom you have given me as a daughter? I am not worthy to be her servant? How shall I handle the true Ark of the Testament? Give me, O my Lord and King, the necessary graces to know your will and to execute it according to your pleasure in the service of my daughter."

The Lord answered that she was to treat her heavenly child outwardly as mothers treat their daughters, without any demonstration of reverence; but to retain this reverence inwardly, fulfilling the laws of a true mother toward her, and rearing her up with all motherly love and care. All this the happy mother complied with; making use of this permission and her mother's rights without losing her reverence, she regaled herself with her most holy daughter, embracing and caressing her in the same way as other mothers do with their daughters. But it was always done with a proper reverence and consciousness of the hidden and divine sacrament known only to the mother and daughter. The guardian angels of the sweet child with others in great multitudes showed their veneration to Mary as she rested in the arms of her mother; they joined in heavenly music, some of which was audible to blessed Anne. The thousand angels appointed as guardians of the great Queen offered themselves to her service. This was also the first time, in which the heavenly Mistress saw them, and Mary asked them to join with her in the praise of the Most High and to exalt Him in her name.

At the moment of the birth of our Princess Mary, the Most High sent the archangel Gabriel as an envoy to bring this joyful news to the holy Fathers in limbo. Immediately the heavenly ambassador descended, illumining that deep cavern and rejoicing the just who were detained there. He told them that already the dawn of eternal felicity had commenced and that the reparation of man, which was so earnestly desired and expected by the holy Patriarchs and foretold by the Prophets, had begun, since she, who was to be the Mother of the Messiah, had now been born; soon they would now see the salvation and glory of the Most High. The holy prince gave them an understanding of the excellence of the most holy Mary and of what the Omnipotent had begun to work in her, in order that they might better comprehend the happy beginning of the mystery, which was to end their prolonged imprisonment. Then all the holy Patriarchs and Prophets and the rest of the just in limbo rejoiced in spirit and in new canticles praised the Lord for this benefit.

All these happenings at the birth of our Queen succeeded each other in a short space of time. The first exercise of her senses in the light of the material sun, was to recognize her parents and other creatures. The arms of the Most High began to work new wonders in her far above all conceptions of men, and the first and most stupendous one was to send innumerable angels to bring the Mother of the eternal Word body and soul into heaven for the fulfilling of His further intentions regarding her. The holy princes obeyed the divine mandate and receiving the child Mary from the arms of her holy mother Anne, they arranged a new and solemn procession bearing heavenward with incomparable songs of joy the true Ark of the Covenant, in order that for a short time it might rest, not in the house of Obededon, but in the temple of the King of Kings and of the Lord of Lords, where later on it was to be placed for all eternity. This was the second step, which most holy Mary made in her life, namely, from this earth to the highest heaven.

On the eighth day after the birth of the great Queen multitudes of most beautiful angels in splendid array descended from on high bearing a shield on which the name of MARY was engraved and shone forth in great brilliancy. Appearing to the blessed mother Anne, they told her, that the name of her daughter was to be MARY, which name they had brought from heaven, and which divine Providence had selected and now ordained to be given to her by Joachim and herself. Anne called for her husband and they conferred with each other about this order of God in regard to the name of their daughter. They both accepted the name with joy and devout affection. They decided to call their relatives and a priest and then, with much solemnity and festivity, they imposed the name of MARY on their child. The angels also celebrated this event with most sweet and ravishing music, which, however, was heard only by the mother and her most holy daughter.

    The sovereign child was treated like other children of her age. Her nourishment was of the usual kind, though less in quantity; and so was her sleep, although her parents sought that she take more sleep. She was not troublesome, nor did she ever cry for mere annoyance, as is done by other children, but she was most amiable and caused no trouble to anybody. That she did not act in this regard as other children caused no wonder; for she often wept and sighed (as far as her age and her dignity of Queen and Mistress would permit) for the sins of the world and for its Redemption through the coming of the Savior. Ordinarily she maintained, even in her infancy, a pleasant countenance, yet mixed with gravity and a peculiar majesty, never showing any childishness. She sometimes permitted herself to be caressed, though, by a secret influence and a certain outward austerity, she knew how to repress the imperfections connected with such affections. Her prudent mother Anne treated her child with incomparable care and caressing tenderness; also Joachim loved her as a father and as a saint, although he was ignorant of the mystery at that time. The child showed a special love toward him, as one whom she knew for her father and one much beloved of God. Although she permitted more tender caresses from her father than from others, yet God inspired the father as well as all others, with such an extraordinary reverence and modesty towards her whom He had chosen for His Mother that even his pure and fatherly affection was outwardly manifested only with the greatest moderation and reserve.

It was ordained therefore by the Most High, that the sovereign child should voluntarily keep this silence during the time in which ordinarily other children are unable to speak. The only exception made was in regard to the conversation held with the angels of her guard, or when she addressed herself in vocal prayer to the Lord. She would pray with her lips and her tongue, but her mother never heard her, nor did she know of her being able to speak during that period; and from this it can be better seen, what perfection it required in her to pass that year and a half of her infancy in total silence. But during that time, whenever her mother freed her arms and hands, the child Mary immediately grasped the hands of her parents and kissed them with great submission and reverent humility, and in this practice she continued as long as her parents lived. She also sought to make them understand during that period of her age, that she desired their blessing, speaking more by the affection of her heart than by word of mouth. So great was her reverence for them, that never did she fail in the least point concerning the honor and obedience to them. Nor did she cause them any trouble or annoyance, since she knew beforehand all their thoughts and was anxious to fulfill them before they were made manifest.

When she reached the age of two years she began to exercise her special pity and charity toward the poor. She sought alms for them from her mother who kindly granted her petitions, both for the sake of the poor and to satisfy the tender charity of her most holy daughter, at the same time encouraging her who was the mistress of mercy and charity, to love and esteem the poor. Besides giving what she obtained expressly for distribution among the poor, she reserved part of her meals for the same purpose, in order that from her infancy it might be said of her more truly than of Job: from my infancy compassion grew with me. She gave to the poor not as if conferring a benefit upon them, but as paying a debt due in justice, saying in her heart: this my brother and master deserves what he needs and what I possess without deserving. In giving alms she kissed the hands of the poor, and whenever she was alone, she kissed their feet, or, if this was impossible, she would kiss the ground over which they passed. Never did she give an alms to the poor without obtaining still greater favors on their souls by interceding for them.

    Even more admirable was the humility and obedience of this holy child in permitting herself to be taught to read and to do other things as other children in that time of life. She was instructed in reading and other arts by her parents and she submitted, though she had infused knowledge of all things created. The angels were filled with admiration at the unparalleled wisdom of this child, who willingly listened to the teaching of all. Her holy mother Anne, as far as her intuition and love permitted, observed with rapture the heavenly princess and blessed the Most High in her. But with her love, as the time for presenting her in the temple approached, grew also the dread of the approaching end of the three years set by the Almighty.

Chapter 3

HOW ST. ANNE AND ST. JOACHIM OBTAINED GOD'S GRACE TO CONCEIVE A CHILD

*Sermon on St. Anne
by Saint Vincent Ferrer*

Saint Anne seeing that she was not able to have a child, sought the four ways that she might have one by the power of God. First, through devout prayers, Second, through giving alms, Third, by many fasts, Fourth, by a vow and promise.

DEVOUT PRAYERS

She went often to the temple to pray, that God might give them the fruit of marriage, because that is the end, -- so trees are planted in the garden, that they might bear fruit -- and they said, "Lord you have placed us in the garden of marriage, etc." And weeping they begged for a child. So on one occasion when St. Anne saw a sparrow's nest in the garden, in tears she said to

God, "O Lord, you have given to this sparrow so many chicks, for which with great labor she provides. Lord give me a child." Behold her first manner of turning to God, by praying, because no one else can give a son or a daughter, for creation is required for that.

Now you have to know that it is the sin of many who when they cannot have a child of their marriage turn to fortune tellers, or nowadays In-Vitro Fertilization, etc. And so repent and confess, and seek from God, because if the fruit of marriage is useful to your soul, know that He shall give it to you. The authority of Christ on this: "Amen, amen I say to you: if you ask the Father anything in my name, he will give it you," (Jn 16:23). Note: **"In my name," which is Jesus, that is, savior. It is asked in the name of the savior when a man ask something useful for salvation, and not for damnation.**

GIVING ALMS

Second, Joachim and Anne begged God for a child through alms, because the angel said to Tobias, "Prayer is good with fasting and alms more than to lay up treasures of gold," (Tob 12:8). And because they were rich, not from usurious interest, but from their possessions. And Jerome says, that he divided his goods into three parts. The first he gave to God. The second to pilgrims, orphans and the poor. The third they kept for themselves and the family's house. Note how he divided his grain: The first part he sent to the temple, the second was set out for the poor, the third for themselves. The same for the wine, the oil and the rest. In this manner prayer is aided by alms, and vice versa. Therefore scripture says, "Give alms out of your substance, and turn not away your face from any poor person: for so it shall come to pass that the face of the Lord shall not be turned from you," (Tob 4:7).

Morally. We find this teaching, that if you are not able to give so much alms as you are bound, nor does the heart suffice, you should pay at least a tenth and first-fruits. There are some who say, "O shall I give my goods to wicked clergymen? Certainly not!" It is said that it is given to God, and not to them. If however God has bad clergy, he shall castigate them, and by this you ought not to hold back from them their right. For if a king has bad soldiers, you ought to not for this reason withhold from him what is due, because someone else would receive the commission for him. So too for God, because, "The earth is the Lord's and the fullness thereof: the world, and all they that dwell therein," (Ps 23:1). And he grants it to us for an annual account, and in a sign of His dominion He keeps for Himself a tenth, but he does not eat it, but gives it to His servants. And when it is paid well, He keeps and conserves it, otherwise all is lost. When you believe you have grain or wine does not God say, "Because you paid me badly, I shall devastate all. And so come storms, hail etc." Therefore Malachi said: "For you afflict me. And you have said: Wherein do we afflict you? In tithes and in first fruits. And you are cursed with want, and you afflict me, even the whole nation of you," (Mal 3:8-9). This is the remedy. "Bring all the tithes into the storehouse, that there may be meat in my house, and try me in this, says the Lord: if I open not unto you the flood-gates of heaven, and pour you out a blessing even to abundance. And I will rebuke for your sakes the devourer," (Mal 3:10-11). If you cannot give as much alms as St. Anne, at least return your thefts, extorted interest, loot, damages and acres. And so James says, " I made good all the damage: whatsoever was lost by theft, you did exact it of me, "(Gen 31:39).

FASTING

Third, they petitioned with fasting, although they were noble and delicate, yet they kept all fasts and precepts and even more, saying, "That from our flesh may proceed the fruit of marriage, let us make the fruit of fasting. And each could say, "I humbled my soul with fasting; and my prayer shall be turned into my bosom," (Ps 34:13).

Morally, you have here the teaching that you should keep the fasts of the church. To this especially are bound those who can have one good meal.

VOWS AND PROMISES

Fourth, they sought a child from God by promises, because together Joachim and Anne made a vow that if God would give them the fruit of marriage, they would serve God in the temple. Just as now if you would promise to become a religious or a nun. But many are damned by promises and vows, making vows and not caring to fulfill them. It is a grave sin to break vows in any way, greater than homicide, because it is unfaithfulness. Therefore the wise man said, " If you have vowed anything to God, defer not to pay it: for an unfaithful and foolish promise displeases him: but whatsoever you have vowed, pay it. And it is much better not to vow, than after a vow not to perform the things promised," (Eccl 5:3-4). When there a definite time is fixed, within which it ought to be fulfilled. If however there is not fixed a determined time, it must be understood that they are to fulfill it immediately.

HOPING FIRMLY

St. Anne bore her fruit, the Virgin Mary, by hoping firmly when it was certified by the angel, whom God sent to her. For which note here the story how Joachim and Anne came from Nazareth to Jerusalem to the temple, to offer according to their custom. When Joachim wished to make an offering, a priest looked at him saying, "And who are you?" He replied, "Father I am Joachim, your servant, who have come to offer sacrifice." And the priest said, "I will certainly not accept your offering, because you are cursed by God, because you do not have a child. It is a sign that there is some hidden sin in you." And Joachim said to him, "Father, I do not know of any great sin in me, although I am not able to be excused of sin, because I do not have a child, and this displeases me very much." And the priest said to him, "Get out of the temple." And Joachim replied, "Father, do not shame me so much."

And the priest said, "Surely, until you get out I will make no offering or sacrifice." Then Joachim, with great shame, left the temple. If a priest wished to act in such a way now, namely expel one of the nobles from church, immediately his knight would say, "By my body this one will die, etc. I shall find him." But Joachim patiently withdrew and he did not return home out of shame because of his neighbors, but he went to his shepherds in the forest, and there, weeping, prayed saying, "O Lord, what is my sin, because I am so accursed." His wife Anne, however, who had been in the temple, when she heard that the priest so contended with her husband, and spurned him, left the temple and went home lest she harm the priest.

Here women have a model, how they should console their husbands who are upset by business, and when they come home, the wives ought to console them. But there are some who do not comfort them, rather sadden them even more. When however St. Anne went home and did not find her husband there, she put aside every creaturely desire from herself, and on bended knees prayed for her holy and just husband that God might keep him. Behold the holy wife. While Joachim so wept praying in the wilderness, the archangel Gabriel appeared to him and Joachim was afraid, because this is the condition of the spirit, for flesh cannot stand the presence of a spirit. But the condition of a good spirit is to comfort immediately, saying to him:

"Behold, your prayers are heard. Because of that patience which you had, God sent me to you, that I might announce to you that you, with your wife shall have a daughter. And as a sign of this, go into Jerusalem, in the golden gate you will find Anne your wife, because I shall announce this to her also."

And the angel withdrew, and appeared to Anne who was weeping at home, because she knew nothing about her husband. The angel spoke well saying that, "You shall be made sorrowful, but your sorrow shall be turned into joy" (Jn 16:20).

Joachim and Anne persisted for twenty years, praying, giving alms, fasting and vowing, and with all this they did not have a child. And because he kept his patience in this shaming inflicted on him by a priest, immediately he had the promise of a child. It follows from this that before God, **patience is better than prayers, alms, fasting or promises. Now think about it, for if you will to have patience in injuries or events, this virtue counts more with God for getting that which you need in this world, and salvation in the other, than anything else.**

Sacred scripture says: "For patience is necessary for you; that, doing the will of God, you may receive the promise" (Heb 10:36).

Chapter 4

ST. ANNE FULFILLS HER PROMISE OF GIVING MARY TO THE TEMPLE

There is no doubt, that she would have lost her life in this fierce and vivid sorrow, if the hand of the Almighty had not comforted her.

    Mary began to prepare her mother, telling her, six months before, her ardent desire of living in the temple. She spoke of the benefits, which they had received at the hands of the Lord, how much they were obliged to seek His greater pleasure, and how, when she should be dedicated to God in the temple, she would be more her daughter than in their own house.

    The holy Anne heard the discreet arguments of her child Mary; but though she was resigned to the divine will and wished to fulfill her promise of offering up her beloved daughter, yet the natural force of her love toward such an unequalled and beloved treasure, joined with the full understanding of its inestimable value, caused a mortal strife in her most faithful heart at the mere thought of her departure, which was closely at hand. There is no doubt, that she would have lost her life in this fierce and vivid sorrow, if the hand of the Almighty had not comforted her: for the grace and dignity of her heavenly daughter was fully known to her and had entirely ravished her heart, making the presence of Mary more dear to her than life. Full of this grief she said to the child: "My beloved daughter, for many years I have longed for Thee and only for a few years do I merit to have thy company; but thus let the will of God be fulfilled; I do not wish to be unfaithful to my promise of sending Thee to the temple, but there is yet time left for fulfilling it: have patience until the day arrives for the accomplishment of your wishes."

At the same time Saint Anne had a vision, in which the Lord enjoined her to fulfill her promise by presenting her daughter in the temple on the very day, on which the third year of her age should be complete. There is no doubt that this command caused more grief in Saint Anne, than that given to Abraham to sacrifice his son Isaac. But the Lord consoled and comforted her, promising His grace and assistance in her loneliness during the absence of her beloved daughter.

Saint Joachim also had a vision of the Lord at this time, receiving the same command as Anne. Having talking with each other and taking account of the will of the Lord, they resolved to fulfill it with humble submission and appointed the day on which the child was to be brought to the temple. Great was also the grief of this holy old man, though not quite as that of Saint Anne, for the high mystery of her being the future Mother of God was still concealed from him.

The Virgin Mary said, "I loved my parents dearly, and the tender words of my mother wounded my heart; but as I knew it to be the will of the Lord to leave them, I forgot her house and my people in order to follow my Spouse. The proper education and instruction of children will do much toward making them more free and used to the practice of virtue, since they will be accustomed to follow the sure and safe guiding star of reason from its first dawn.

The three years' time decreed by the Lord having been completed, Joachim and Anne set out from Nazareth, accompanied by a few kindred and bringing with them the true living Ark of the Covenant, the most holy Mary, borne on the arms of her mother in order to be deposited in the holy temple of Jerusalem. The beautiful child, by her fervent and loving aspirations, hastened after the ointments of her Beloved, seeking in the temple Him, whom she bore in her heart. This humble procession was scarcely noticed by earthly creatures, but it was invisibly accompanied by the angelic spirits, who, in order to celebrate this event, had hastened from heaven in greater numbers than ordinary as her bodyguard, and were singing in heavenly strains the glory and praise of the Most High. The Princess of heaven heard and saw them as she hastened her beautiful steps along in the sight of the highest and the true Solomon. Thus they pursued their journey from Nazareth to the holy city of Jerusalem, and also the parents of the holy child Mary felt in their hearts great joy and consolation of spirit.

They arrived at the holy temple, and the blessed Anne on entering took her daughter and mistress by the hand, accompanied and assisted by Saint Joachim. All three offered a devout and fervent prayer to the Lord; the parents offering to God their daughter, and the most holy child, in profound humility, adoration and worship, offering up herself. She alone perceived that the Most High received and accepted her, and, amid divine splendor which filled the temple, she heard a voice saying to her:

"Come, my Beloved, my Spouse, come to my temple, where I wish to hear thy voice of praise and worship."

Having offered their prayers, they rose and took themselves to the priest. The parents gave their child into his hands and he gave them his blessing. Together they took her to the portion of the temple buildings, where many young girls lived to be brought up in retirement and in virtuous habits, until old enough to assume the state of matrimony.

Fifteen stairs led up to the entrance of these apartments. Other priests came down these stairs in order to welcome the blessed child Mary. The one that had received them, being according to the law one of a minor order, placed her on the first step. Mary, with his permission, turned and kneeling down before Joachim and Anne, asked their blessing and kissed their hands, recommending herself to their prayers before God. The holy parents in tenderness and tears gave her their blessing; whereupon she ascended the fifteen stairs without any assistance. She hastened upward with incomparable fervor and joy, neither turning back, nor shedding tears, nor showing any childish regret at parting from her parents. To see her, in so tender an age, so full of strange majesty and firmness of mind, excited the admiration of all those present. The priests received her among the rest of the girls, and Saint Simeon consigned her to the teachers, one of whom was the prophetess Anne. This holy woman had been prepared by the Lord by special grace and enlightenment, so that she joyfully took charge of this child of Joachim and Anne. She considered the charge a special favor of divine Providence and merited by her holiness and virtue to have her as a disciple, who was to be the Mother of God and Mistress of all creatures.

      Sorrowfully her parents Joachim and Anne retraced their journey to Nazareth, now poor as deprived of the rich Treasure of their house. But the Most High consoled and comforted them in their affliction. The holy priest Simeon, although he did not at this time know of the mystery enshrined in the child Mary, obtained great light as to her sanctity and her special selection by the Lord; also the other priests looked upon her with great reverence and esteem. In ascending the fifteen stairs the Child brought to fulfillment, that, which Jacob saw happening in sleep; for here too were angels ascending and descending: the ones accompanying, the others meeting their Queen as She hastened up; whereas at the top God was waiting in order to welcome her as His daughter and spouse. She also felt by the effects of the overflowing love, that this truly was the house of God and the portal of heaven.

When the heavenly child Mary had left her parents and entered upon her life in the temple, her teacher assigned to her a place among the rest of the girls, each of whom occupied a little room. The Princess of heaven prostrated herself on the pavement, and, remembering that it was holy ground and part of the temple, she kissed it. In humble adoration she gave thanks to the Lord for this new benefit, and she thanked even the earth for supporting her and allowing her to stand in this holy place; for she held herself unworthy of treading and remaining upon it. Then she turned toward her holy angels and said to them: "Celestial princes, messengers of the Almighty, most faithful friends and companions, I ask you with all the powers of my soul to remain with me in this holy temple of my Lord and as my vigilant sentinels, reminding me of all that I should do; instructing me and directing me as the teachers and guides of my actions, so that I may fulfill in all things the perfect will of the Most High, give pleasure to the holy priests and obey my teacher and my companions." And also addressing the twelve angels of the Apocalypse, she said: "And I beseech you, my ambassadors, if the Almighty permit you, go and console my holy parents in their affliction and solitude."

Chapter 5

THE DEATHS OF ST. ANNE AND ST. JOACHIM

The Virgin Mary gave praise to the Most High for the infinite mercies, which He had shown to her mother both in life and in death.

The Most High said to Mary, "Beautiful art thou in your thoughts, Daughter of the Prince, my Dove, my beloved and chosen one. I accept your desires as highly pleasing to me and according to my divine will, thy father Joachim must pass from this mortal to the eternal and immortal life. His death will happen shortly and he will pass in peace and shall be placed among the saints in limbo, to await the Redemption of the human race." This announcement did not disturb the royal heart of the princess of heaven, the blessed Mary; but as the love of children for their parents is a just debt of nature, and as in this most holy child this love had attained its highest perfection, the natural sorrow for the loss of her father Joachim could not be wanting, for she loved him with a holy love. The tender and sweet child therefore felt, that this sorrowful compassion was perfectly compatible with the serenity of her magnanimous heart, and, working in all things with grandeur, giving nature and grace each their due, she offered an ardent prayer for her father Saint Joachim. She asked the Lord to give him grace to depend upon Him as his powerful and true God in his transit through a blessed death; and asked Him to defend Joachim against the demon especially in that hour, preserve him for and constitute him among the number of the elect, since during his life he had confessed and magnified His admirable and holy name. And in order to oblige His Majesty the more, the most faithful Daughter offered to suffer all that the Lord might ordain. The Lord accepted this petition and consoled the heavenly Child by assuring her, that He would assist her father as a most merciful and kind rewarder of those that love and serve Him, and that He would place him among the Patriarchs Abraham, Isaac and Jacob. At the same time He prepared her anew for the acceptance and endurance of troubles. Eight days before the death of the Patriarch Joachim the most holy Mary received another notice from the Lord, advising her of the day and hour in which he was to die. His death took place only six months after her entrance into the temple. Having received this notice from the Lord, She requested the twelve angels, mentioned by Saint John in the Apocalypse, to assist her father Joachim and to comfort and console him in his sickness, which they did. For the last hours of his life she sent all the angels of her guard asking the Lord, to make them visible to him for his greater consolation. God conceded this favor and confirmed all the wishes of His chosen and only one; and the great patriarch, most happy Joachim, saw the thousand angels which guarded Mary. In response to her prayer and wishes the Almighty allowed his graces to overflow, commanding the angels to address Joachim as follows:

"Man of God may the Most High and powerful Lord be thy eternal salvation and may He send thee from His holy place the necessary and opportune help for thy soul. Mary thy daughter has sent us in order to assist you in this hour, in which you must pay the debt of mortality to your Creator. She is a most faithful and powerful intercessor before the Almighty, in whose name and peace you will now pass consoled and joyous from this world, because He has made thee the father of such a blessed daughter. Mary, thy Daughter, is chosen and ordained by the Almighty as the One, in whom the divine Word shall vest Himself with human flesh and form. She is to be the happy Mother of the Messiah and the Blessed among women, the most exalted among all creatures, and only inferior to God Himself. Your most fortunate daughter is to restore what the human race lost by the first sin, and she is the high mountain on which is to be established the new law of grace. Since you leave to the world a daughter, through whom God will restore it and prepare a full remedy, part from it in the joy of your soul, and may the Lord bless thee from Sion and constitute you in the inheritance of the saints and bring you to the vision and enjoyment of the blessed Jerusalem."

During these words of the holy angels to Joachim, his spouse, holy Anne, stood at the head of his bed and by divine disposition she heard and understood what they said. In the same moment the holy patriarch lost the use of speech and, treading into the path common to all flesh, he commenced his agony in a marvelous struggle between his joy at this message and the pain of death. In this conflict of the interior powers of his soul he made many fervent acts of divine love, of faith, of admiration, of praise, of thanksgiving, of humility and heroic acts of many other virtues. Thus absorbed in the knowledge of so divine a mystery, he arrived at the term of his natural life and died the precious death of the saints. His holy soul was carried by the angels to the limbo of the Patriarchs and just souls and, for a new consolation and light in the protracted night in which they lived, the Most High sent the soul of Joachim as the last messenger and legate of the Lord to announce to the whole congregation of the just that the dawn of the eternal day was at hand; that the morning light was breaking upon the world in most holy Mary, Daughter of Joachim and Anne; that from her was to be brought forth the Sun of the Divinity, Christ, the Redeemer of all the human race. This great news the holy fathers and the just in limbo heard and received with jubilee and in their exultation they sang many hymns of thanksgiving to the Most High.

When Mary reached the age of twelve years, the holy angels, spoke to her saying: "Mary, the end of the life of your holy mother Anne as ordained by the Most High, is now about to arrive, and His Majesty has resolved to free her from the prison of her mortal body and bring her labors to a happy fulfillment."

At this unexpected and sorrowful message the heart of the affectionate daughter was filled with compassion. Prostrating Herself in the presence of the Most High, She poured forth a fervent prayer for the happy death of her mother Saint Anne in the following words: "King of the ages, invisible and eternal Lord, immortal and almighty Creator of the universe, although I am but dust and ashes and although I must confess, that I am in debt to your greatness, I will not on that account be prevented from speaking to my Lord, and I pour out before you my heart, hoping, 0 my God, that Thou wilt not despise her, who has always confessed your holy name. Dismiss, 0 Lord, in peace thy servant, who has with invincible faith and confidence desired to fulfill your divine pleasure. Let her issue victoriously and triumphantly from the hostile combat and enter the portal of your holy chosen ones; let your powerful arm strengthen her; at the close of her mortal career, let that same right hand, which has helped her to walk in the path of perfection, assist her, and let her enter, 0 my Father, into the peace of your friendship and grace, since she has always sought after it with an upright heart."

The Lord did not respond expressly in words to this petition of His beloved; but His answer was a marvelous favor, shown to her and to her mother, Saint Anne. During that night His Majesty commanded the guardian angels of the most holy Mary to carry her bodily to the sickbed of her mother and one of them to remain in her stead, assuming for this purpose an aerial body a substitute for hers. The holy angels obeyed the mandate of God and they carried Mary to the house and to the room of her holy mother Anne. Being thus brought to the presence of her mother, she kissed her hand and said to her: My mother and mistress, may the Most High be your light and your strength, and may He be blessed, since He has in His condescension not permitted me in my necessity to remain without the benefit of your last blessing: may I then receive it, my mother, from your hand." Holy Anne gave her last blessing to Mary and with overflowing heart also thanked the Lord for the great favor conferred upon herself. For she knew the sacrament of her daughter and queen, and she did not forget to express her gratitude for the love, which Mary had shown her on this occasion.

In the midst of such exalted and heavenly graces, Saint Anne felt the throes of death approaching and, reclining upon the throne of grace, that is, in the arms of her most holy daughter Mary, she rendered her most pure soul to her Creator. Having closed the eyes of her mother, the Queen Mary was again taken up by the holy angels and restored to her place in the temple. The Most High did not impede the force of her filial love, which naturally would cause a great and tender sorrow at the death of her mother and a sense of loneliness at being deprived of her assistance. But these sorrows were most holy and perfect in our Queen, governed by the graces of her most prudent innocence and purity. In the midst of them she gave praise to the Most High for the infinite mercies, which He had shown to her mother both in life and in death.

Chapter 6

Devotion to Saint Anne through the Ages

"The privilege of aiding men in every distress has been given to good Saint Anne."
~St. Thomas Aquinas

Devotion to Saint Anne began as soon as the first Disciples and Apostles started to spread the Gospel throughout the world. The remains of the Saints and Martyrs are always very important to Catholics and all altars have the remains of at least one martyr within them. They also may contain relics from a Saint especially if the altar is dedicated to them.[i]

So the mortal remains of the Grandmother of God are some of the greatest relics ever. The Apostles and Disciples took Jesus' command to go out into all the world and spread the Gospel. Lazarus, Mary Magdalen, and Martha were all under considerable persecution at the time and the Pharisees and Sadducees plotted to kill

Lazarus because he was raised from the dead by Jesus. They formed one of the first missionary groups with their cousin Maximin and Jesus' cousins as well as St. Anne's nieces Mary Jacobe and Mary Salome. This group brought with them the most precious thing they wanted to protect and keep, the mortal remains of St. Anne which was placed in a coffer fashioned from cedar wood and they travelled to Marseilles(called Massilia at the time), France where Lazarus would become the first Bishop there.[ii]

    The sisters would eventually set up nearby helping the people of a small fishing village to get closer to Jesus. Maximin set up his mission in the small town of Apt with the help of Martha. The apostolate of Lazarus was very successful and he was able to build a firm foundation for the Diocese that he ran for a long time. His successor Bishops kept the most precious relics there but in time the invasions in the area threatened to destroy the city and the relics would be lost perhaps forever. The Bishop of the time met in council with other members of the church and decided that the relics of Saint Anne would be safer in the Bishopric of Apt and the relics were transferred there. The coffer with the remains was placed inside a more substantial one and placed under lock and key. Soon it was felt even this would be not enough to protect these holy relics and they were moved to a secret part of the catacombs next to the cathedral with no markings left to give away the position except a symbolic sculpting that a trained observer would know meant St. Anne's relics were left there. Soon after hiding the relics in 576 AD, the whole city was left for ruin by the invading army of Lombards. The relics were hidden just in time, to be returned to the church in miraculous fashion over a hundred years later by the great king Charlemagne.[iii] There is an amazing story told by Archbishop Dubreil of Avignon:

"It is related that Charlemagne, having concluded one of his many expeditions, had returned to Apt. But it is not known whether his visit was for the purpose of placing his sword beside that of Caesar on the coat of arms of Apt or of being present at the consecration of the cathedral. As this church was one of the forty churches he had promised to build if victory crowned his expeditions, it would seem that Providence wished him to be present as a witness of the miraculous discovery of the relics. On Easter Sunday in the year 792, the Emperor assisted at the Divine Office, surrounded by the faithful and his knights. Suddenly, a youth, blind and a deaf-mute from birth, son of a lord of the place named Caseneuve de Simiane, came into the church like one inspired and led by an invisible hand. The congregation, evidently also inspired, immediately rose up instinctively and followed him to the steps of the sanctuary. By gestures he requested a stone slab to be lifted and the place to be dug up. The Emperor, who shared in the general excitement, ordered the boy to be obeyed. Accordingly, the stone was removed and digging was begun, and soon the crypt was discovered where lay the relics, and whence bright rays issued.

"Through an opening the cypress coffer was seen, and a bright light illumined the place. Then a prodigy was witnessed which is worthy of being is recalled side by side with that by which the True Cross was recognized by St. Helena. The young man, suddenly cured, cried out: 'It is she.' The same words were repeated by the people who fell on their knees and broke into tears. In fact the coffer was found a winding sheet, that enclosed the relics, on which were inscribed those words that dispelled all doubt: 'Here lies the body of St. Anne, Mother of the Glorious Virgin Mary.'"

After this amazing find there was great rejoicing in the city of Apt which would then be known as the final resting place of Saint Anne. Charlemagne took a portion of the relics to Aix la Chapelle, gave some to friends and a report to the Pope and leaving the major portion as well as the ossuary in the hands of the Bishop of Apt and his successors.[iv]

Saint Anne first major church built in her honor was in Constantinople around 550 AD and another church was built for her in Jerusalem at the site of her home in 636 AD. After these two many other churches spread throughout the Near East and then spread westward toward Europe. Now there are chapels and churches in her honor built throughout the whole world.

What the Saints have to Say about Saint Anne:

"St. Anne by her intercession drives out depression and evil thoughts. She also aids the poor, cures the sick and comforts the sorrowing. She removes tribulations and by her intercession obtains for her clients the grace to eradicate vice and implant virtue. She obtains light for the intellect, strength for the will and affection for the heart. This powerful Saint has preserved thousands from contagious diseases. Through

her intercession, evil spirits have been expelled. For the barren in the married state, she obtains children and Heavenly assistance in delivery. She inspires the despairing with trust in God's mercy and excites the tepid to zeal and fervor. St. Anne has rescued many from imminent death; yes, through her intercession the dead have, in several instances, been restored to life.
Those who worthily venerate St. Anne can obtain aid in every necessity through her mediation."
~Abbot Trithemius

"We believe that St. Anne continually intercedes for us with the merciful Lord, for through her great benefits have come to mankind. From her was born the ever pure and immaculate Virgin Mary, who was found worthy to bring forth Jesus Christ, our Redeemer."
~Pope Gregory XIII

"We do not doubt that the more love we show to the mother of Mary, the more we merit the intercession and aid of the holy Virgin who brought forth the only-begotten Son of God, Our Lord Jesus Christ."
~Pope Gregory XV

"We know and are convinced that our good mother St. Anne helps in all needs, dangers and tribulations, for Our Lord wishes to show us that He will do also in Heaven
what she asks of Him for us."
~St. Teresa of Avila

"Approach St. Anne, your amiable protectress, with full confidence. Knock at her gates with persevering prayer, because she can obtain for you the forgiveness of your sins and can open Heaven for you. She lacks nothing that can profit you ... Believe me, who has already obtained many a favor through her whom the Queen of Heaven honors as her dearest mother

...No one knows, no one believes, how many favors God confers on lovers of Saint Anne!"
~Abbot Trithemius

"Saint Anne is a generous mother, because the word 'Anne' means 'generous, merciful, gracious.'"
~St. John Damascene

The privilege of aiding men in every distress has been given to good Saint Anne.
~St. Thomas Aquinas

In desperate cases of need, I always invoke the holy mother Anne.
~Venerable Catherine Emmerich

My Devotion to Saint Anne

My devotion to Saint Anne began when I read "Good Saint Anne" by Tan Books that inspired me to have a greater devotion to her and I highly recommend it. After reading the book I obtained two great graces through her intercession. The first grace was my pastor and spiritual director had me wait for a period of time before I could consecrate myself to Mary through "True Devotion to Mary" by St. Louis De Montfort. I wanted this grace so badly especially because I had to wait. I believe that is why God worked through Father Eric to have me wait so long. The longer I waited the more I wanted the grace. Then, I remembered Saint Anne and how she could obtain anything from her daughter, Mary and her grandson Jesus. Well, I began to pray to her and promised to buy 150-200 of the Good Saint Anne books to distribute if she answered my prayers. Of course she did very quickly and before I knew it I had been consecrated to Mary and I continue to do my best to remain Mary's good servant and child every day. The grace of consecration I believe is one of the greatest I have ever received and I owe it all to Saint Anne's intercession. Soon

Father Eric had 150-200 books to distribute at his parish and it took him several years to give them all away and we both laughed about it. The second great grace was my daughter Sarah had a small limp and inward turn to her leg as a baby. My wife and I prayed to St. Anne to intercede for us and soon after treatment she was all healed and completely normal. In thanksgiving we went on pilgrimage a few years later to, you guessed it, St. Anne De Beaupre which is an amazing place. So very breathtakingly beautiful and soul inspiring. We left the leg brace that we got for our daughter which she no longer needed as a testimonial to Saint Anne's powerful intercession. I highly recommend you make the pilgrimage whenever you can to this most spiritual place and I am sure you will have many stories of your own to add as well as graces received there. It has been many years since we went there and I cannot wait to go back. Now I have an opportunity to thank Saint Anne again by writing this book in her honor and to inspire everyone to become her grandchildren as she will shower her grandchildren with so many graces. God bless you!

Chapter 7

Saint Anne de Beaupre Shrine: A Place of Miracles

"There, the paralytics walk, the blind can see, and the sick are healed of every kind of illness.
~ Marie de l'incarnation

Saint Anne de Beaupré is a small town and contains the greatest basilica dedicated to Saint Anne in the world. Along the beautiful and picturesque Saint Lawrence River north of Quebec this town was settled around 1650. Shortly after the first chapel was built to Saint Anne, when shipwrecked French sailors had promised to build her a chapel if they survived the storm. They kept their promise and during the first day of the building of the small chapel the first of many, many miracles occurred. [v]

Saint Anne showed her appreciation for the building of the chapel by healing Louis Guimont, a resident of the town who had a very painful rheumatoid arthritis. He placed three stones in the chapel's foundation and trusted in her prayerful assistance and his confidence was rewarded when he was completely cured. This amazing miracle inspired many others to come to Saint Anne De Beaupre to receive their own miracles and the flow of pilgrims to this amazing shrine has not stopped since with millions upon millions of people coming to be healed of too many illnesses to record. Within a few years of the building of this chapel a sister Marie de l'incarnation said in 1665, "Seven leagues from here, there is a village called "The Little Cape", where there is a church dedicated to Saint Anne in which Our Lord is working great marvels in favor of the holy mother of the Most Blessed Virgin Mary. **There, the paralytics walk, the blind can see, and the sick are healed of every kind of illness**."

      The Basilica of Saint Anne De Beaupre was rebuilt many times and the last one was completed in 1963 and is an amazingly beautiful shrine and Basilica and is known as a place of miracles. The main wall at the entry of the basilica is covered with canes, crutches and other aids as testimony of their healings received.[vi]

The Shrine has three notable relics from Saint Anne.

The first relic is a portion of the bone of Saint Anne's finger was received on March 12, 1670. The second relic arrived at the Shrine on July 26, 1892, as a gift from Pope Leo XIII. It is a 4-inch portion of the bone of Saint Anne's forearm. The last relic of Saint Anne is from her forearm and arrived as a gift from Blessed Pope John XXIII and was received on July 3, 1960.[vii]

Some of favors granted through Saint Anne's intercession:

Wonderful New Work Situation

One man came to the shrine in 1980 on a pilgrimage to obtain help at work which was getting progressively worse due to regular harassment against him there. This caused him to become depressed and he even had to leave work for a few weeks to obtain some relief. As he was coming to the shrine all the way there it was dark and cloudy. When he was able to see the shrine a bright shining light suddenly shone between the two bell towers and he took this as a sign of hope. After spending a day at the shrine in prayer and enjoying the most beautiful shrine he returned home and the very next day he was offered a new job. Twenty eight years later he retired from the same wonderful job and he returned to Beaupre to thank good Saint Anne for her powerful intercession. Amazing Grace!

The Blessing of Children

A Couple came to the shrine to ask Saint Anne to obtain the favor of children for them. As they were leaving the young woman asked Saint Anne if she would have children someday. At that exact moment she saw a double rainbow over the Saint Lawrence River and she knew then that God would bless them with not just one child but two! Two years later she felt called by Saint Anne to meet her daughter the Virgin Mary at Medjugorje and a few years later after thirteen years of Marriage they had their first daughter on September 8, Mary the Mother of God's Birthday. Soon after they had a second daughter and they hope to return to Saint Anne at her shrine soon! Amazing Grace!

Eczema of the Worst Kind Cured

A woman was afflicted with the worst kind of eczema imaginable. Her skin would literally peel off her arms and was excruciatingly painful. She had been treated by many doctors with no help, even going as far as New York City to see a specialist to no avail. She was not even able to dress herself because of the pain. Where medical doctors had no help, she turned to Saint Anne and went on pilgrimage to her shrine. While there she applied a pink colored ointment but only for a moment as she thought it might hurt her. However after that she began to feel better and better. Over some time her eczema was slowly and completely cured, never to return!

Foot saved from amputation

A man who worked in the construction business contracted an infection of some sort that left his entire foot black and the doctors told him that unless the disease subsided they would have to amputate the foot. He had some friends in Quebec who heard about his ailment and sent him a bottle of Saint Anne's oil and a prayer to be recited daily. Every night he would put the oil on the foot and pray the prayers and soon his foot was completely healed and he was able to return to work!

Incurable Heart Disease CURED!

A woman went to St. Anne de Beaupre on pilgrimage with her son who had been diagnosed with an incurable heart disease and told that he had only a little time left to live. After she took her son to the hospital and all his symptoms had disappeared. Incurable was cured!

Four to Six Months to Live
(Seven years later ALIVE!)

A woman was told by her doctor after an operation that she had only four to six months left to live from the stomach cancer afflicting her. After praying to Saint Anne she is still alive today! Her doctor told her children that she is a "small miracle"

Walking Again!

A young boy was very afflicted by the disease Muscular Dystrophy that confined him to a wheelchair and left his spine crooked. A risky operation was proposed to straighten the back using steel rods. He promised to bring his brace to Saint Anne de Beaupre if the operation was a success. Of course it was a success and he came to the shrine with twenty of his relatives to give thanks as now he can stand up and take a few steps out of the wheelchair and is much improved beyond all expectations. The brace is now placed with many, many others on the north pillar of the Basilica.

Excruciating Spine Pain

One woman came to the shrine having great pain in her spine for many years in which she could hardly bend or lift anything. She participated in the Novena to Saint Anne and a candlelight procession as well as venerated the relic of Saint Anne. Shortly after this all her pains went away and she was cured of this grievous pains.

Lung Cancer Cured!

"On October 18, 2006, I was diagnosed with lung cancer. My family and I were very discouraged. After a few days, I decided not to give up. I began radiation therapy and chemotherapy in November 2006. I finished my treatments in March 2007. I began to pray to Good Saint Anne every day and we went to the Shrine several times with my husband, my two children and my sisters. I prayed with all my heart to the Infant Jesus, Holy Mary, Saint Joseph and Saint Anne. Last week, on June 15, 2007, I had a CAT scan at the Laval Hospital in Quebec City. The doctor assured me that I was cured; I realized in my heart that Saint Anne had performed a miracle for me and I thanked her immediately. I told the doctor that we are very happy about this good news. We will continue to pray to Good Saint Anne every day for what she has done for me.

Stomach Cancer Cured!

"I would like to share what, in my view, is a miracle in modern times. On June 1, 2006, my husband found out that he had stomach cancer, one of the most violent cancers, with a chance of survival for five years after the operation, with the risk of losing his voice if it became necessary to remove the esophagus. THE WHOLE FAMILY WAS DEVASTATED. We have two girls and three grandchildren and we have been married for 35 years… Life was good. We have faith in God and we are practicing Catholics. My husband had great confidence and a profound devotion to Saint Anne. We went to the Basilica to pray, but my husband cried and was unable to pray. A COUPLE IS STRONG. I decided to help him and asked him to let himself be carried by Saint Anne and the light of our God. At our church, at home, with brothers and sisters, friends and neighbors,

I asked that everyone wear the armor of the light and love of God because we were going to war against this enemy that was cancer. OPERATION. I waited close to the door; I was seated and not doing anything when a lady stopped and said to me, "I sense the presence of God in you; could I support you?" I had not noticed the time passing. I think the Good God sent me an angel in this woman. The presence of God was felt in her with the power to have an effect. The operation lasted 10 hours. He lost consciousness three times. They removed his esophagus and stomach. The surgeon told me that he would have a lot of suffering; he may not speak again. CONVALESCENCE. My husband had no postoperative pain and has still kept his beautiful voice. He eats what he wants and is doing very well. From time to time the doctor asks, "The pain? " – "I don't have any. ". One day the doctor said, "Perhaps there is a part that belongs to GOD!" CONCLUSION. My husband has just finished his radiation treatment and chemotherapy. We don't know if the cancer will come back but this trial has united the whole family. My husband chose to teach the love and presence of God during his convalescence. He feels pains and joys in a new way since he has a new life. Without Saint Anne my husband would perhaps be gone today.

Miracle Baby!

"My son and his wife just had a "miracle baby". In 1989, they had a boy and in 1994 a girl, but there were then some difficult pregnancies and deaths at birth. When they learned they were expecting a new child they immediately went to Saint Anne de Beaupré; they asked the good Saint Anne to protect it. He arrived in good health. On July 26, 2007, the whole family – and Jimmy, the newborn - came to thank the Good Saint Anne.

Faith Enkindled and Life Lengthened!

"About 15 years ago I often travelled from Nova Scotia to Ontario. I always used the Autoroute 20 but by luck (or destiny) one day I decided to take Highway 138. When I got to Saint Anne de Beaupré, I had to fill up with gas and stopped at a gas station not far from the shrine. Attracted by the splendor of this building I decided to go and see what it was like inside. I immediately felt a sacred presence. I stayed for some time, I had read a bit about Saint Anne, I recited several prayers, a lit a candle and continued on my way. Every day since that day, each time I go by Quebec City I would take Highway 138, so I could make a visit to Saint Anne de Beaupré. Years later, in May 2004, I was diagnosed with cancer. The doctors told me that I had this cancer for 2 or 3 years, but I had not been sick or had any symptom of its presence. They told me the cancer had become very malignant and that I had less than six months to live. I was appalled. I was afraid of dying and afraid of the impact this news would have on my wife and our son. I did not know where to turn and decided to go to Saint Anne de Beaupré. I made the journey by car and spend close to a day alone in prayer. I opened my heart to Saint Anne and asked her to spare my life. I also prayed for the strength to face the events and for my fears to be calmed if I should die. When initially diagnosed that my condition was so serious I was not even offered a treatment and after some months my condition deteriorated dramatically. In October 2004 the doctors decided to do an operation but advised me that it would certainly not be a cure. It is now three years since the first diagnosis. The doctors recently told me that my cancer is still there but it is borrowed time. I feel well and am no longer afraid for my life. I feel obliged to present my testimony of thanks to Sainte-Anne-de-Beaupré, by reference to this mysterious joy that I discovered in your church. What is strange is that I am not even Catholic. I was born in England and belong to the Anglican

Church. But I think that neither Saint Anne nor the Good God nor Jesus Christ loves me any the less for that. I would appreciate very much if you would keep me, my wife Pauline and our son Matthieu in your prayers. May God bless you, the priests and the people in your parish for this Shrine of Hope, this place where prayers are heard!

It's a place where miracles can happen and actually occur.[viii]

Saint Anne is patroness of unmarried women, housewives, women in labor, grandmothers, horseback riders, cabinet-makers. Saint Anne is also the patron saint of sailors and a protector from storms. [ix]

Chapter 8

PRAYERS TO ST. ANNE

"The honor you show to my mother is doubly dear and pleasing to me."
-Our Lady

St Anne Prayer (To Obtain Some Special Favor)

Glorious St. Anne, filled with compassion for those who invoke you and with love for those who suffer, heavily laden with the weight of my troubles, I cast myself at your feet and humbly beg of you to take the present affair which I recommend to you under your special protection.

St. Anne, please, recommend to your daughter, the Blessed Virgin Mary, and lay it before the throne of Jesus, so that He may bring it to a happy issue.

St. Anne cease not to intercede for me until my request is granted. (Here ask for favor you wish to obtain.)

Above all, obtain for me the grace of one day beholding my God face to face, and with you and Mary and all the saints, praising and blessing Him through all eternity. Amen.

Good St. Anne, mother of her who is our life, our sweetness and our hope, pray to her for us and obtain our request. (Three times).

Parents Prayer to St. Anne

We call upon you, dear St. Anne, for help in bringing up our family in good and godly ways. Teach us to trust God our Father as we rear the precious heritage entrusted to us. May His will prevail in our lives and His providence defend us. These blessings we ask for all families in our neighborhood, our country, and our world. Amen.

Children's Prayer to St. Anne

Good St. Anne, you must have loved your parents just like we love Mom and Dad. They love us so much and take care of all our needs. Help us to make them happy every day. Thank you, dear Grandmother of Jesus, for listening to our prayer. Amen.[x]

Grandchildren of Saint Anne

The Grandchildren of Saint Anne was formed to have everyone adopt Saint Anne as our grandmother. Through this adoption we are sure to obtain many, many graces as she is the mother of the "Mother of All Graces" and through her intercession we are sure to obtain all that we ask for as long as it is in the most loving, merciful will of God. Devotion to Saint Anne is second only to devotion to Saint Joseph and Our Lady among faithful Catholics since the beginning of the church. Our Lady herself told one of her servants to add to her daily Rosary, One Our Father and One Hail Mary in honor of Saint Anne, Our Lady's holy mother. She also said, **"Those who honor Saint Anne will obtain great aid in every need, especially at the hour of death."** Our Lady also said to another, **"The honor you show to my mother is doubly dear and pleasing to me."** Our Lady appeared to a hermit who was filled with bitter anguish of spirit and prayed to her for help, Our Lady said, "Since you are lovingly devoted to me, I will take away all your grief and sorrow of soul, **but I admonish you to venerate and praise my dear mother also, if you desire great graces from me.** I am highly pleased with the affection accorded to my beloved mother. **Know too, that my Son, Jesus, has promised to deliver from misfortune all who honor my mother and to assist them in attaining eternal glory. My son, practice this devotion and make it known."**

Daily Prayers for the Grandchildren of Saint Anne

Memorare to Saint Anne

Remember, O Good Saint Anne, whose name means grace and mercy, that never was it know that anyone who fled to your protection, implored your help, and sought your intercession, was left unaided. Inspired with this confidence, I come before you, sinful and sorrowful. Holy mother of the Immaculate Virgin Mary, and loving grandmother of the Savior, do not reject my appeal, but hear me and answer my prayer. Amen

Grandchildren of Saint Anne's Prayer

Saint Anne, please adopt me as your grandchild, Love me as you love Jesus and Mary, pray for me as your grandchild, and always be my consoler, my advocate. Reconcile me to God. Console me in all my trials; strengthen me in my struggles. Deliver me from danger in my time of need. Help me at the hour of death and open to me the gates of paradise. Also pray for all the intentions of your Grandchildren throughout the world (state your intention). We ask this all in the Name of Jesus and His Holy Mother Mary, Amen.

O, Jesus, Holy Mary, Saint Anne, help me now and at the hour of my death. Amen
Pray an Our Father and Hail Mary

To join all you need to do is pray these prayers every day and sign up:
An Our Father, Hail Mary, the Memorare to Saint Anne and the Grandchildren of Saint Anne Prayer.

Become a Grandchild of Saint Anne today at ThePoweroftheRosary.com

Chapter 9

Prayer

He who prays is certainly saved. He who prays not is certainly damned.
~St. Alphonsus Liguori

Extracted from: THE GREAT MEANS OF SALVATION AND OF PERFECTION by St. Alphonsus Liguori

He who prays is certainly saved. He who prays not is certainly damned. All the blessed (except infants) have been saved by prayer. All the damned have been lost through not praying; if they had prayed, they would not have been lost. And this is, and will be, their greatest torment in hell, to think how easily they might have been saved, only by asking God for His grace; but that now it is too late, -- the time of prayer is over.

Prayers are so dear to God, that he has appointed the angels to present them to Him as soon as they come forth from our mouths. 'The angels,' says St. Hilary, 'preside over the prayers of the faithful, and offer them daily to God.' This is that smoke of the incense, which are the prayers of saints, which St. John saw ascending to God from the hands of the angels (Rev. 8:3); and which he saw in another place represented by golden vials full of sweet odors, very acceptable to God. But in order to understand better the value of prayers in God's sight, it is sufficient to read both in the Old and New Testaments the innumerable promises which God makes to the man that prays. Cry to me, and I will hear you (Ps. 49,15). Call upon me, and I will deliver you (Jer. 33,3). Ask, and it shall be given you; seek, and you shall find; knock, and it shall be opened to you. He shall give good things to them that ask him (Mt. 7,7). Everyone that asks receives, and he that seeks finds (Lk. 11,10). Whatsoever they shall ask, it shall be done for them by my Father (Jn 15,7). All things whatsoever you ask when you pray, believe that you shall receive them, and they shall come to you (Mt. 18,19). If you ask me anything in my name, that will I do (Jn 14,14). You shall ask whatever you will, and it shall be done to you. Amen, amen, l say to you, if you ask the Father anything in my name, he will give it to you (Jn 16,23). There are a thousand similar texts; but it would take too long to quote them.

God wills us to be saved; but for our greater good, he wills us to be saved as conquerors. While, therefore, we remain here, we have to live in a continual warfare; and if we should be saved, we have to fight and conquer. 'No one can be crowned without victory,' says St. Chrysostom. We are very feeble, and our enemies are many and mighty; how shall we be able to stand against them, or to defeat them? Let us take courage, and say with the Apostle, I can do all things in him who strengthens me (Phil. 4,13). By prayer we can do all things; for by this means God will give us that strength which we want. Theodoret says, that **prayer is omnipotent; it is but one, yet it can do all things**: 'Though prayer is one, it can do all things.' And St. Bonaventure asserts that **by prayer we obtain every good,**

and. escape every evil: 'By it is obtained the gain of every good, and liberation from every evil.' St. Laurence Justinian says, that by means of prayer we build for ourselves a strong tower, where we shall be secure from all the snares and assaults of our enemies: 'By the exercise of prayer man is able to erect a citadel for himself:' 'The powers of hell are mighty,' says St. Bernard; 'but **prayer is stronger than all the devils.**' Yes; for by prayer the soul obtains God's help, which is stronger than any created power. Thus David encouraged himself in difficulties: Praising I will call upon the Lord, and I shall be saved from my enemies (Ps. 17,3). For, as St. Chrysostom says, 'Prayer is a strong weapon, a defense, a port, and a treasure.' It is a weapon sufficient to overcome every assault of the devil; it is a defense to preserve us in every danger; it is a port where we may be safe in every tempest; and it is at the same time a treasure which provides us with every good.

God knows the great good which it does us to be obliged to pray, and therefore permits us to be assaulted by our enemies, in order that we may ask him for the help which he offers and promises to us. But as he is pleased when we run to him in our dangers, so is he displeased when he sees us neglectful of prayer. 'As the king,' says St. Bonaventure, 'would think it faithlessness in an officer, when his post was attacked, not to ask him for reinforcements, he would be reputed a traitor if he did not request help from the king'; so God thinks himself betrayed by the man who, when he finds himself surrounded by temptations, does not run to him for assistance. For **he desires to help us; and only waits to be asked, and then gives abundant help.**

Come to me, all you that labor and are burdened, and I will refresh you (Mt. 11,28). 'My poor children,' says our Savior, 'though you find yourselves assailed by enemies, and oppressed with the weight of your sins, do not lose heart but have recourse to me in prayer, and I will give you strength to resist, and I will give you a remedy for all your disasters.' In another place he says, by the mouth of Isaiah, Come and accuse me, says the Lord; if your sins be as scarlet, they shall be made white as snow (Is. 1,18). O men, come to me; though your consciences are horribly defiled, yet come; I even give you leave to reproach me (so to speak), if after you have had recourse to me, I do not give you grace to become white as snow.

What is prayer? It is, as St. Chrysostom says, 'the anchor of those tossed on the sea, the treasure of the poor, the cure of diseases, the safeguard of health.' It is a secure anchor for him who is in peril of shipwreck; it is a treasury of immense wealth for him who is poor; it is a most efficacious medicine for him who is sick; and it is a certain preservative for him who would keep himself well. What does prayer effect? Let us hear St. Laurence Justinian: 'It pleases God, it gets what it asks, it overcomes enemies, it changes men.' It appeases the wrath of God, who pardons all who pray with humility. It obtains every grace that is asked for; it vanquishes all the strength of the tempter, and it changes men from blind into seeing, from weak into strong, from sinners into saints. Let him who wants light ask it of God, and it shall be given. As soon as I had recourse to God says Solomon, he granted me wisdom: I called upon, and the Spirit of wisdom came to me (Wis. 7,7). Let him who wants fortitude ask it of God, and it shall be given. As soon as I opened my mouth to pray, says David, I received help from God: I opened my mouth, and drew in the Spirit (Ps. 118,131). And how in the world did the martyrs obtain strength to resist tyrants, except by prayer, which gave them force to overcome dangers and death?

'He who uses this great weapon,' says St. Chrysostom, 'knows not death, leaves the earth, enters heaven, lives with God.' He falls not into sin; he loses affection for the earth; he makes his abode in heaven; and begins, even in this life, to enjoy the conversation of God. How can you even bother a man by saying: 'How do you know that you are written in the book of life?' How do you know whether God will give you efficacious grace and the gift of perseverance? Be not solicitous, says St. Paul, but in everything by prayer and supplications, with thanksgiving, let your petitions be known to God (Phil. 4,6). What is the use, says the Apostle, of agitating yourselves with these miseries and fears? Drive all these cares from you, which are of no use but to lessen your confidence, and to make you more tepid and slothful in walking along the way of salvation. Pray and seek always, and make your prayers sound in God's ears, and thank him for having promised to give you the gifts which you desire whenever you ask for them, namely efficacious grace, perseverance, salvation, and everything that you desire. **The Lord has given us our post in the battle against powerful foes; but He is faithful in His promises, and will never allow us to be assaulted more violently than we can resist: God is faithful, who will not suffer you to be tempted above that which thou are able**

(I Cor. 10,13). He is faithful, since he instantly helps the man who prays to Him. Cardinal Gotti writes that God has bound Himself not only to give us grace precisely balancing the temptation that assails us, but that He is obliged, when we are tempted, and have recourse to Him, to afford us, by means of that grace which is kept ready for and offered to all, sufficient strength for us actually to resist the temptation. 'God is bound, when we are tempted, and fly to His protection, to give us by the grace prepared and offered to all such strength as will not only put us in the way of being able to resist, but will also make us resist; "for we can do all things in Him who strengthens us" by His grace, if we humbly ask for it.' We can do all things with God's help, which is granted to everyone who humbly seeks it; so that we have no excuse when we allow ourselves to be overcome by a temptation. We are conquered solely by our own fault, because we would not pray. **By prayer all the snares and power of the devil are easily overcome.** 'By prayer all hurtful things are chased away,' says St. Augustine...**Prayer is a treasure; he who prays most receives most.**

St. Bonaventure says that every time a man has recourse to God by fervent prayer, he gains good things that are of more value than the whole world: **'Any day a man gains more by devout prayer than the whole world is worth.'** Some devout souls spend a great deal of time in reading and in meditating, but pay but little attention to prayer. There is no doubt that spiritual reading, and meditation on the eternal truths, are very useful things; 'but,' says St. Augustine, 'it is of much more use to pray.' **By reading and meditating we learn our duty; but by prayer we obtain the grace to do it.** 'It is better to pray than to read: by reading we know what we ought to do; by prayer we receive what we ask.' What is the use of knowing our duty, and then not doing it, but to make us more guilty in God's sight? Read and meditate as we like, we shall never satisfy our obligations, unless we ask of God the grace to fulfil them.

And, therefore, as St. Isidore observes, the devil is never more busy to distract us with the thoughts of worldly cares than when he perceives us praying and asking God for grace: 'Then mostly does the devil insinuate thoughts, when he sees a man praying.' And why? Because the enemy sees that at no other time do we gain so many treasures of heavenly goods as when we pray. This is the chief fruit of mental prayer, to ask God for the graces which we need for perseverance and for eternal salvation; and chiefly for this reason it is that mental prayer is morally necessary for the soul, to enable it to preserve itself in the grace of God. For if a person does not remember in the time of meditation to ask for the help necessary for perseverance, he will not do so at any other time; for without meditation he will not think of asking for it, and will not even think of the necessity for asking it. On the other hand, he who makes his meditation every day will easily see the needs of his soul, its dangers, and the necessity of his prayer; and so he, will pray, and will obtain the graces which will enable him to persevere and save his soul. Father Segneri said of himself, that when he began to meditate, he aimed rather at exciting affections than at making prayers. But when he came to know the necessity and the immense utility of prayer, he more and more applied himself, in his long mental prayer, to making petitions.

As a young swallow so will I cry, said the devout king Hezekias (Is. 38,14). The young of the swallow does nothing but cry to its mother for help and for food; so should we all do, if we would preserve our life of grace. We should be always crying to God for aid to avoid the death of sin, and to advance in his holy love. Father Rodriguez relates that the ancient Fathers, who were our first instructors in the spiritual life, held a conference to determine which was the exercise most useful and most necessary for eternal salvation; and that they determined it was to repeat over and over again the short prayer of David, Incline unto my aid, O God! (Ps. 69,1) .

'This,' says Cassian 'is what everyone ought to do who wishes to be saved: he ought to be always saying, My God, help me! my God, help me!' We ought to do this the first thing when we awake in the morning; and then to continue doing it in all our needs, and when attending to our business, whether spiritual or temporal; and most especially when we find ourselves troubled by any temptation or passion. St. Bonaventure says that at times we obtain a grace by a short prayer sooner than by many other good works: 'Sometimes a man can sooner obtain by a short prayer what he would be a long time obtaining by pious works' St. Ambrose says that he who prays, while he is praying obtains what he asks, because the very act of prayer is the same as receiving: 'He who asks of God, while he asks receives; for to ask is to receive.' Hence St. Chrysostom wrote that **'there is nothing more powerful than a man who prays,'** because such a one is made partaker of the power of God. To arrive at perfection, says St. Bernard, we must meditate and pray: by meditation we see what we want; by prayer we receive what we want. 'Let us mount by meditation and prayer: the one teaches what is deficient, the other obtains that there should be nothing deficient.'

In conclusion, to save one's soul without prayer is most difficult, and even (as we have seen) impossible, according to the ordinary course of God's providence. But **by praying our salvation is made secure, and very easy.** It is not necessary in order to save our souls to go among the heathen, and give up our life. It is not necessary to retire into the desert, and eat nothing but herbs. **What does it cost us to say, My God, help me! Lord, assist me! have mercy on me! Is there anything more easy than this? and this little will suffice to save us, if we will be diligent in doing it.** St. Laurence Justinian specially exhorts us to oblige ourselves to say a prayer at least when we begin any action: 'We must endeavor to offer a prayer at least in the beginning of every work.' Cassian attests that the principal advice of the ancient Fathers was to have recourse to God with short but frequent prayers. Let no one, says St. Bernard, think lightly of prayer, because God values it, and then gives us either what we ask, or what is still more useful to us: 'Let no one undervalue his prayer, for God does not undervalue it . . . **he will give either what we ask, or what he knows to be better.'** And let us understand, that if we do not pray, we have no excuse, because the grace of prayer is given to everyone. It is in our power to pray whenever we will, as David says of himself: With me is prayer to the God of my life; I will say to God, you are my support (Ps 41,8 9).

God gives to all the grace of prayer, in order that thereby they may obtain every help, and even more than they need, for keeping the divine law, and for persevering till death. If we are not saved, the whole fault will be ours; and we shall have our own failure to answer for, because we did not pray.[xi]

Saint Quotes on Prayer

A soul arms itself by prayer for all kinds of combat. In whatever state the soul may be, it ought to pray. A soul which is pure and beautiful must pray, or else it will lose its beauty; a soul which is striving after this purity must pray, or else it will never attain it; a soul which is newly converted must pray, or else it will fall again; a sinful soul, plunged in sins, must pray so that it might rise again. There is no soul which is not bound to pray, for **every single grace comes to the soul through prayer.**

--St. Faustina

Prayer is an aspiration of the heart, it is a simple glance directed to heaven, it is a cry of gratitude and love in the midst of trial as well as joy; finally, it is something great, supernatural, which expands my soul and unites me to Jesus.

--St.Therese of Lisieux

"Pray as though everything depended on God. Work as though everything depended on you."
--St. Augustine

You pay God a compliment by asking great things of Him.
--St. Teresa of Avila

It is simply impossible to lead, without the aid of prayer, a virtuous life.
--Saint John Chrysostom

Virtues are formed by prayer. Prayer preserves temperance. Prayer suppresses anger. Prayer prevents emotions of pride and envy. Prayer draws into the soul the Holy Spirit, and raises man to Heaven.
--Saint Ephraem of Syria

"Purity is the fruit of prayer."
- St. Mother Teresa

Prayer is the place of refuge for every worry, a foundation for cheerfulness, a source of constant happiness, a protection against sadness.
--St. John Chrysostom

The most potent and acceptable prayer is the prayer that leaves the best effects. I don't mean it must immediately fill the soul with desire . . . The best effects [are] those that are followed up by actions-----when the soul not only desires the honor of God, but really strives for it.
--St. Teresa of Avila

'He who prays most receives most.'
--St. Alphonsus Maria de Liguori

My little children, your hearts, are small, but prayer stretches them and makes them capable of loving God. Through prayer we receive a foretaste of heaven and something of paradise comes down upon us. Prayer never leaves us without sweetness. It is honey that flows into the

souls and makes all things sweet. **When we pray properly, sorrows disappear like snow before the sun.**
--Saint John Vianney

"Private prayer is like straw scattered here and there: If you set it on fire it makes a lot of little flames. But gather these straws into a bundle and light them, and you get a mighty fire, rising like a column into the sky; public prayer is like that."
--Saint John Vianney

"Somebody who says his Rosary alone only gains the merit of one Rosary, but if he says it together with thirty other people he gains the merit of thirty Rosaries. This is the law of public prayer. How profitable, how advantageous this is!"~St Louis De Montfort

'We must speak to God as a friend speaks to his friend, servant to his master; now asking some favor, now acknowledging our faults, and

communicating to Him all that concerns us, our thoughts, our fears, our projects, our desires, and in all things seeking His counsel.'
--St. Ignatius of Loyola

During mental prayer, it is well, at times, to imagine that many insults and injuries are being heaped upon us, that misfortunes have befallen us, and then strive to train our heart to bear and forgive these things patiently, in imitation of our Savior. This is the way to acquire a strong spirit.
--St. Philip Neri

How often I failed in my duty to God, because I was not leaning on the strong pillar of prayer.
--St. Teresa of Avila

Don't imagine that, if you had a great deal of time, you would spend more of it in prayer. Get rid of that idea; it is no hindrance to prayer to spend your time well.
--St. Teresa of Avila

Jacob did not cease to be a Saint because he had to attend to his flocks.
--St. Teresa of Avila

Prayer ought to be humble, fervent, resigned, persevering, and accompanied with great reverence. One should consider that he stands in the presence of a God, and speaks with a Lord before whom the angels tremble from awe and fear.
--Saint Mary Magdalen de Pazzi

We must pray without tiring, for the salvation of mankind does not depend upon material success . . . but on Jesus alone.
--St. Frances Xavier Cabrini

"The prayer most pleasing to God is that made for others and particularly for the poor souls. Pray for them, if you want your prayers to bring high interest."

--Blessed Anne Catherine Emmerich

One must not think that a person who is suffering is not praying. He is offering up his sufferings to God, and many a time he is praying much more truly than one who goes away by himself and meditates his head off, and, if he has squeezed out a few tears, thinks that is prayer.
--St. Teresa of Avila

"Much more is accomplished by a single word of the Our Father said, now and then, from our heart, than by the whole prayer repeated many times in haste and without attention."
--Saint Teresa of Avila

My daughter...why do you not tell me about everything that concerns you, even the smallest details? **Tell Me about everything, and know that this will give Me great joy.** I answered, But You know about everything, Lord." And Jesus replied to me, "Yes I do know; but you should not

excuse yourself with the fact that I know, but with childlike simplicity talk to Me about everything, for my ears and heart are inclined towards you, and your words are dear to Me.
~Jesus to Saint Faustina

Without Prayer nothing good is done. God's works are done with our hands joined, and on our knees. Even when we run, we must remain spiritually kneeling before Him.
--Blessed Luigi Orione

We must pray without ceasing, in every occurrence and employment of our lives - that prayer which is rather a habit of lifting up the heart to God as in a constant communication with Him.
--Saint Elizabeth Anne Seton

Prayer ought to be short and pure, unless it be prolonged by the inspiration of Divine grace.
--Saint Benedict

"Have confidence in prayer. It is the unfailing power which God has given us. By means of it you will obtain the salvation of the dear souls whom God has given you and all your loved ones." Ask and you shall receive," Our Lord said. Be yourself with the good Lord."

--Saint Peter Julian Eymard[xii]

Prayer in my Life

When this chapter on prayer came up and I wanted to write about it I felt a little unqualified as I do not consider myself a great prayer person or anything. However, I do take the promises of the Lord and Our Lady and really attach myself to them. Thus, when I read the promises of the Rosary, I really, really attach myself to them. Then I pray the Rosary a lot because well for one reason, I will obtain all I ask for. WOW! This seems like too great of a deal to me. Once I came back to the Lord after leaving Him for atheism for many years, I really came back to Him as much as I could. Especially through the Power of the Rosary. So I have been praying the Rosary for almost 20 years now and I can tell you that I have obtained everything I have been praying for so far and of course I have many, many more prayers so I know I will receive all the promises as well. I see myself as Jacob wrestling with God and I will not let Him go. What do I pray for, I pray for all good, my basic intentions are the Healing, Conversion, Salvation of the whole world especially all my spiritually adopted brothers and sisters. Second is for all our family's missions and projects such as Dolls from Heaven spreading throughout the world. Third, the healing of my family and all those on my sick list. Fourth, working for God's Glory as a family without financial difficulties full time exclusively. Fifth, release of all the Holy Souls in Purgatory. Sixth, peace in America and the whole world, Seventh, the End of Abortion, Contraception, and Euthanasia, Seven basic intentions and I am sure

I will obtain them all because God is great all the time.

So besides the Rosary I pray: the Memorare. St. Gertrude's prayer, which I pray to release souls from purgatory. (The Releasers). Also Divine Mercy for the Dying, The Dolorians prayer, Army of the Face of Jesus prayer, and all my prayer groups from ThePowerofTheRosary.com. These prayers all have great promises attached to them and are very powerful and they give me great confidence that I will receive all God promises.

Also my favorite short prayer is: Jesus, Mary, and Joseph, I love you save souls, and take care of everything. I pray this one all the time as much as I can. I am very simple in praying, I ask God for what I want and I trust that I will receive it. That being said I feel like my prayers are never answered in the way I expect them to be, they are always answered even better than I could have imagined. I always have a vision for the future and God always exceeds that vision. I have no rose colored glasses. I know suffering comes with everything but through prayer the suffering comes easier than I could ever have hoped for. Somehow, I roll with the punches life throws at me. Today for example was perhaps one of the happiest days of my life but also one of my most depressing as I just felt the weight of the world crashing down on me. Prayer and work pulled me through. Instead of focusing on how bad I felt, I prayed and worked my way through it and now I am here writing this to you and I hope it will give you some strength to see that through prayer and work you will change the whole world. Yes, **You will change the whole world**. "Become who God wants you to be and you will set the whole world on Fire!"

~St. Catherine of Sienna

Chapter 10

GRANDPARENTS

"Grandparents are a Treasure!"
~Pope Francis

I am hoping to inspire all grandparents to follow in the footsteps of the greatest role model of grandparents, St. Anne and St. Joachim. It does not matter if you have biological or just spiritual grandchildren. To be a grandparent is much more of a spiritual mission than a physical one anyway. I think it closely resembles Godparents as well. Your main mission as a grandparent is to make sure your grandchildren join you in heaven. One wonderful way is to pray the Rosary everyday and after each decade pray this special prayer, "With these beads bind my children "and grandchildren" to your Immaculate Heart." Our Lady will attend to their souls. - St. Louise de Marillac Also pray to Saint Anne that you will be the best grandparent you can be by the grace of

God. For some inspiration I found these beautiful quotes on grandparents:

A child needs a grandparent, anybody's grandparent, to grow a little more securely into an unfamiliar world. – Charles and Anne Morse

What children need most are the essentials that grandparents provide in abundance. They give unconditional love, kindness, patience, humor, comfort, lessons in life. And, most importantly, cookies. – Rudy Giuliani

Grandfathers are for loving and fixing things. ~Unknown

Nobody can do for little children what grandparents do. Grandparents sort of sprinkle stardust over the lives of little children. – Alex Haley

Grandmas and grandpas are grand-angels. – Terri Guillemets

It's such a grand thing to be a mother of a mother — that's why the world calls her grandmother. ~Unknown

Grandma always made you feel she had been waiting to see just you all day and now the day was complete. – Marcy DeMaree

A grandmother is a little bit parent, a little bit teacher, and a little bit best friend. ~Unknown[xiii]

Pope Francis on Grandparents

Let us pray for our grandfathers and grandmothers who often played a heroic role in handing on the faith in times of persecution. Especially in times past, when fathers and mothers often were not at home or had strange ideas, confused as they were by the fashionable ideologies of the day, **grandmothers were the ones who handed on the Faith**".

"Grandparents are a treasure".
"the elderly pass on history, doctrine, faith and they leave them to us as an inheritance. They are like a fine vintage wine; that is, they have within themselves the power to give us this noble inheritance".

The remembrance of our ancestors leads us to imitate their faith. It is true that old age is at times unpleasant, because of the illnesses it brings. But the wisdom of our grandparents is the inheritance we ought to receive. A people that does not care for its grandparents, that does not respect its grandparents, has no future since it has lost its memory.[xiv]

Grandparents in my Life

For me my real grandparents did not get to be so close to me for various reasons (because three of them died before I grew up). That being said I had the greatest grandmother in the person of my great aunt who we all called "Cioci" She was my grandmother's sister and when my grandmother passed away when I was only nine years old she became for me the best grandmother anyone could have asked for. I always think of this quote a lot in regards to her, "Do the Job, get the Title" Well, my Cioci did the job of being my grandmother and thus she gets the title. She was always there to push me to be better and always supported me financially as well. She was tough too as when I messed up she was there to knock me back into place. I know now she is in heaven praying for me and supporting our family like every grandmother does in heaven. **Making sure their grandchildren join them in heaven is grandparents' most important job.** So if you do not have grandchildren, it does not mean you cannot be the greatest grandmother. Remember do the job and you get the title. Find someone in your family or friends families who needs a grandmother or grandfather and start doing the job for them. You will be more appreciated because it will be unexpected. We expect grandparents to be amazing and they usually are, we do not expect them to be someone who is not actually the grandparent.

I have another observation which is that I believe all those who are converted or keep the faith have "great" grandparents that are praying for them. For me it must have been my grandparents in heaven for three passed before I was ten years old. Also my Cioci and my Godmother who is a Catholic nun now in heaven prayed hard I am sure as well as my parents. Those powerful prayers plus the prayers of my brother Eric who died after only living 24 hours, must have prayed hard for this "too smart for his own good" brother who believed in nothing for some time. The truth of Eric's prayers sounded in my heart when I realized that the priest who led me back to the faith has the same name,

Father Eric. He gave me the Rosary and good pamphlets that after praying and reading I have not turned back and never will, God willing till I am in heaven!

Notes

[i] Wikipedia: Altar in the Catholic Church
https://en.wikipedia.org/wiki/Altar_in_the_Catholic_Church

[ii] St. Anne,: Grandmother of Our Savior Hardcover – 1955 by Frances Parkinson Keyes (Author)

[iii] ibid

[iv] Good Saint Anne By Rev. Lawrence G. Lovasik, S.V.D. Divine Word Missionary

[v] Britannica: Saint Anne de Beaupre
https://www.britanneica.com/place/Sainte-Anne-de-Beaupre-Quebec

[vi] Wikipedia: Saint Anne de Beaupre
https://en.wikipedia.org/wiki/Sainte-Anne-de-Beaupr%C3%A9

[vii] Sainte Anne de Beaupre: Relics
https://sanctuairesainteanne.org/en/saint-anne/relics

[viii] Sainte Anne de Beaupre: Favors Granted :
http://www.sanctuairesainteanne.org/favors_granted

[ix] WikiPedia Saint Anne
https://en.wikipedia.org/wiki/Saint_Anne

[x] Saint Anne http://www.saintanne.com/saint-anne/

[xi] The Great Means of Salvation and Perfection by St. Alphonso Liguori
http://www.catholicbible101.com/thepowerofprayer.htm

[xii] White Lily of Trinity, Saint Quotes on Prayer:
http://www.whitelilyoftrinity.com/saints_quotes_prayer.html

[xiii] 50 Great Happy Grandparents Day Quotes
https://sayingimages.com/grandparents-day-quotes/

[xiv] POPE FRANCIS, Grandpa's table Tuesday, 19 November 2013
https://w2.vatican.va/content/francesco/en/cotidie/2013/documents/papa-francesco-cotidie_20131119_grandpa-table.html

Bibliography

Agreda, Maria: Mystical City of God, https://archive.org/stream/mysticalcityofgo01dejauoft/mysticalcityofgo01dejauoft_djvu.txt

Britannica: Saint Anne de Beaupre https://www.britanneica.com/place/Sainte-Anne-de-Beaupre-Quebec

Good Saint Anne By Rev. Lawrence G. Lovasik, S.V.D. Divine Word Missionary

POPE FRANCIS, Grandpa's table Tuesday, 19 November 2013
https://w2.vatican.va/content/francesco/en/cotidie/2013/documents/papa-francesco-cotidie_20131119_grandpa-table.html

Saint Anne http://www.saintanne.com/saint-anne/

Sainte Anne de Beaupre: Favors Granted :
http://www.sanctuairesainteanne.org/favors_granted

Sainte Anne de Beaupre: Relics
https://sanctuairesainteanne.org/en/saint-anne/relics

St. Anne,: Grandmother of Our Savior Hardcover – 1955 by Frances Parkinson Keyes (Author)

THE GREAT MEANS OF SALVATION AND OF PERFECTION by St. Alphonsus Liguori
http://www.catholicbible101.com/thepowerofprayer.htm

White Lily of Trinity, Saint Quotes on Prayer:
http://www.whitelilyoftrinity.com/saints_quotes_prayer.html

_____

Wikipedia: Altar in the Catholic Church
https://en.wikipedia.org/wiki/Altar_in_the_Catholic_Church

Wikipedia: Saint Anne de Beaupre
https://en.wikipedia.org/wiki/Sainte-Anne-de-Beaupr%C3%A9

WikiPedia Saint Anne
https://en.wikipedia.org/wiki/Saint_Anne

50 Great Happy Grandparents Day Quotes
https://sayingimages.com/grandparents-day-quotes/

Other Books by Brian Kiczek

Available at:

MyCatholicFamilyMagazine.com

About the Author

Brian Kiczek, D.C., is a chiropractor, husband, and father of three, who reverted back to the Catholic faith after around ten years of atheism. He is a United States Navy Veteran of the Persian Gulf War. He is popularly known as the Rosary Doctor for his tireless work in spreading the message of the Rosary to anyone open to hear it. He strives to repay the Lord Jesus Christ, for having been merciful to him, in particularly through the power and love of the Immaculate Heart of the Blessed Virgin Mary. He is the cofounder of Dolls from Heaven, My Catholic Family Magazine, and The End of Abortion Movement. He also is the founder of numerous prayer groups like Decade a Day Disciples, The Dolorians, The Releasers, Grandchildren of Saint Anne, and the website, ThePowerofTheRosary.com

www.ingramcontent.com/pod-product-compliance
Lightning Source LLC
LaVergne TN
LVHW011121090325
805511LV00033B/1357